QUIETING your heart

30-DAY PRAYER JOURNAL

darlene schacht

Find Darlene Schacht on the web here:
Blog: TimeWarpWife.com
Facebook: timewarpwife
Twitter: timewarpwife
Pinterest: timewarpwife

Love

1 Corinthians 13:4-12, NIV

Love is patient, love is kind. It does not envy, it does not boast, it is not proud. It does not dishonor others, it is not self-seeking, it is not easily angered, it keeps no record of wrongs. Love does not delight in evil but rejoices with the truth. It always protects, always trusts, always hopes, always perseveres.

Love never fails. But where there are prophecies, they will cease; where there are tongues, they will be stilled; where there is knowledge, it will pass away.

For we know in part and we prophesy in part, but when completeness comes, what is in part disappears. When I was a child, I talked like a child, I thought like a child, I reasoned like a child. When I became a man, I put the ways of childhood behind me.

For now we see only a reflection as in a mirror; then we shall see face to face. Now I know in part; then I shall know fully, even as I am fully known.

TODAY'S PRAYER

_____
_____
_____
_____
_____
_____
_____
_____
_____
_____
_____
_____
_____

By this shall all men know that ye are my disciples, if ye have love one to another. John 13:35

Welcome

DAY 1

TODAY I'M READING

GOD IS...

3 THINGS I'M THANKFUL FOR

THIS IS WHAT I LEARNED TODAY

TODAY'S PRAYER

As the Father hath loved me, so have I loved you: continue ye in my love.
John 15:9

DAY 2

TODAY I'M READING

GOD IS...

3 THINGS I'M THANKFUL FOR

THIS IS WHAT I LEARNED TODAY

TODAY'S PRAYER

_____
_____
_____
_____
_____
_____
_____
_____
_____
_____
_____
_____
_____
_____
_____

Greater love hath no man than this, that a man lay down his life for his friends.
John 15:13

DAY 3

TODAY I'M READING

GOD IS...

3 THINGS I'M THANKFUL FOR

THIS IS WHAT I LEARNED TODAY

This is my commandment, That ye love one another, as I have loved you. John 15:12

DAY 4

TODAY I'M READING

GOD IS...

3 THINGS I'M THANKFUL FOR

THIS IS WHAT I LEARNED TODAY

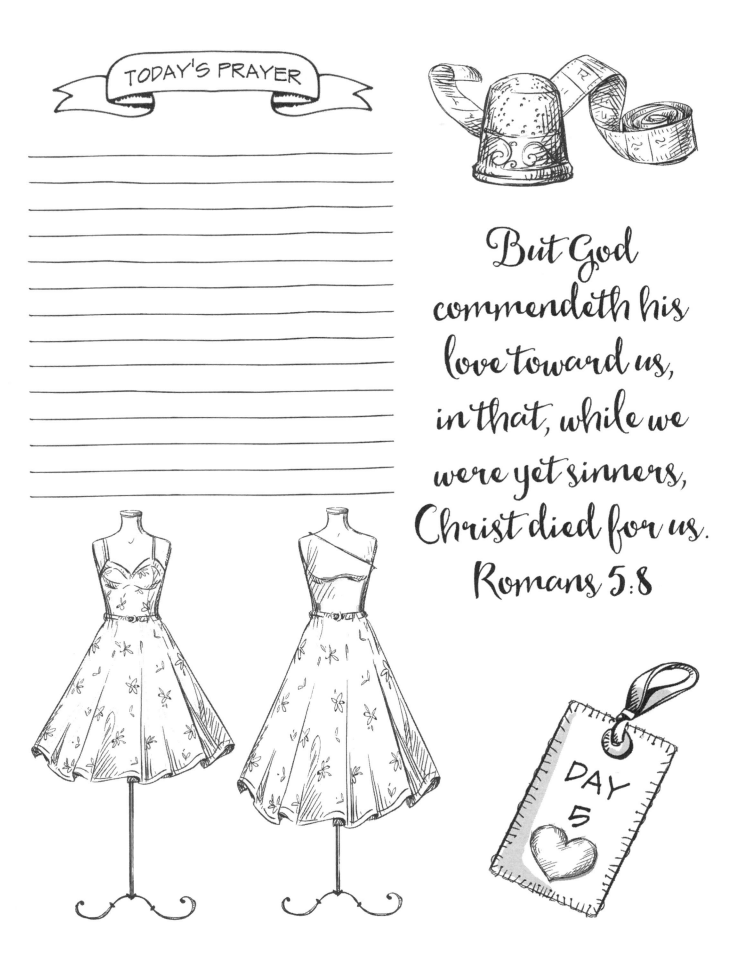

TODAY'S PRAYER

But God commendeth his love toward us, in that, while we were yet sinners, Christ died for us. Romans 5:8

DAY 5

TODAY I'M READING

GOD IS...

3 THINGS I'M THANKFUL FOR

THIS IS WHAT I LEARNED TODAY

TODAY'S PRAYER

Love worketh no ill
to his neighbour:
therefore love is
the fulfilling
of the law.
Romans 13:10

DAY
6

TODAY I'M READING

GOD IS...

3 THINGS I'M THANKFUL FOR

THIS IS WHAT I LEARNED TODAY

GOD IS LOVE

He that loveth not knoweth not God; for God is love.
1 John 4:8

DAY 7

TODAY I'M READING

GOD IS...

3 THINGS I'M THANKFUL FOR

THIS IS WHAT I LEARNED TODAY

TODAY'S PRAYER

Beloved, let us love one another: for love is of God; and every one that loveth is born of God, and knoweth God.
1 John 4:7

DAY 8

TODAY I'M READING

GOD IS...

3 THINGS I'M THANKFUL FOR

THIS IS WHAT I LEARNED TODAY

TODAY'S PRAYER

_____
_____
_____
_____
_____
_____
_____
_____
_____
_____
_____
_____

And thou shalt love the LORD thy God with all thine heart, and with all thy soul, and with all thy might.
Deuteronomy 6:5

HONEY

DAY 9

TODAY I'M READING

GOD IS...

3 THINGS I'M THANKFUL FOR

THIS IS WHAT I LEARNED TODAY

TODAY'S PRAYER

Peace be to the brethren, and love with faith, from God the Father and the Lord Jesus Christ. Ephesians 6:23

DAY 10

TODAY I'M READING

GOD IS...

3 THINGS I'M THANKFUL FOR

THIS IS WHAT I LEARNED TODAY

TODAY'S PRAYER

And above all these things put on charity, which is the bond of perfectness. Colossians 3:14

DAY 11

TODAY I'M READING

GOD IS...

3 THINGS I'M THANKFUL FOR

THIS IS WHAT I LEARNED TODAY

And the Lord make you to increase and abound in love one toward another, and toward all men, even as we do toward you.

1 Thessalonians 3:12

DAY 12

TODAY I'M READING

GOD IS...

3 THINGS I'M THANKFUL FOR

THIS IS WHAT I LEARNED TODAY

TODAY'S PRAYER

Now the end of the commandment is charity out of a pure heart, and of a good conscience, and of faith unfeigned:
1 Timothy 1:5

DAY 13

TODAY'S PRAYER

With all lowliness and meekness, with longsuffering, forbearing one another in love. Ephesians 4:2

DAY 14

TODAY I'M READING

GOD IS...

3 THINGS I'M THANKFUL FOR

THIS IS WHAT I LEARNED TODAY

TODAY'S PRAYER

The love of God is shed abroad in our hearts by the Holy Ghost which is given unto us.
Romans 5:5

DAY 15

TODAY I'M READING

GOD IS...

3 THINGS I'M THANKFUL FOR

THIS IS WHAT I LEARNED TODAY

Charity suffereth long, and is kind; charity envieth not.
1 Cor. 13:4a

Story of our Love

DAY 16

TODAY I'M READING

GOD IS...

3 THINGS I'M THANKFUL FOR

THIS IS WHAT I LEARNED TODAY

TODAY'S PRAYER

Charity vaunteth not itself, is not puffed up, 1 Cor. 13:4b

DAY 17

TODAY I'M READING

GOD IS...

3 THINGS I'M THANKFUL FOR

THIS IS WHAT I LEARNED TODAY

TODAY'S PRAYER

Let love be without dissimulation. Abhor that which is evil; cleave to that which is good. Romans 12:9

DAY 18

TODAY I'M READING

GOD IS...

3 THINGS I'M THANKFUL FOR

THIS IS WHAT I LEARNED TODAY

TODAY'S PRAYER

I beseech you, brethren, for the Lord Jesus Christ's sake, and for the love of the Spirit, that ye strive together with me in your prayers to God for me.

Romans 15:30

DAY 19

TODAY I'M READING

GOD IS...

3 THINGS I'M THANKFUL FOR

THIS IS WHAT I LEARNED TODAY

For, brethren, ye have been called unto liberty; only use not liberty for an occasion to the flesh, but by love serve one another. Galatians 5:13

DAY 20

TODAY I'M READING

GOD IS...

3 THINGS I'M THANKFUL FOR

THIS IS WHAT I LEARNED TODAY

TODAY'S PRAYER

But thou, O man of God, flee these things; and follow after righteousness, godliness, faith, love, patience, meekness.
1 Timothy 6:11

DAY 21

TODAY I'M READING

GOD IS...

3 THINGS I'M THANKFUL FOR

THIS IS WHAT I LEARNED TODAY

TODAY'S PRAYER

_____
_____
_____
_____
_____
_____
_____
_____
_____
_____
_____

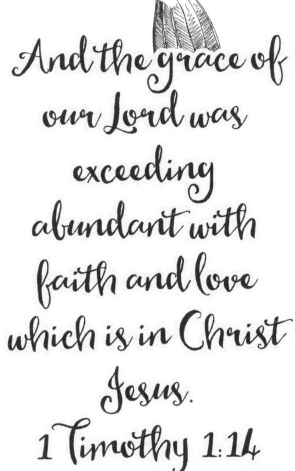

And the grace of our Lord was exceeding abundant with faith and love which is in Christ Jesus.
1 Timothy 1:14

DAY 22

TODAY I'M READING

GOD IS...

3 THINGS I'M THANKFUL FOR

THIS IS WHAT I LEARNED TODAY

Holy Bible

For God hath not given us the spirit of fear; but of power, and of love, and of a sound mind.

2 Timothy 1:7

DAY 23

TODAY I'M READING

GOD IS...

3 THINGS I'M THANKFUL FOR

THIS IS WHAT I LEARNED TODAY

Owe no man any thing, but to love one another: for he that loveth another hath fulfilled the law.
Romans 13:8

I ♥ Coffee

DAY 24

TODAY I'M READING

GOD IS...

3 THINGS I'M THANKFUL FOR

THIS IS WHAT I LEARNED TODAY

TODAY'S PRAYER

Behold, what manner of love the Father hath bestowed upon us, that we should be called the sons of God.
1 John 3:1

DAY 25

TODAY I'M READING

GOD IS...

3 THINGS I'M THANKFUL FOR

THIS IS WHAT I LEARNED TODAY

TODAY'S PRAYER

With all lowliness and meekness, with longsuffering, forbearing one another in love. Eph. 4:2

DAY 26

TODAY I'M READING

GOD IS...

3 THINGS I'M THANKFUL FOR

THIS IS WHAT I LEARNED TODAY

TODAY'S PRAYER

My little children, let us not love in word, neither in tongue; but in deed and in truth. 1 John 3:18

DAY 27

TODAY I'M READING

GOD IS...

3 THINGS I'M THANKFUL FOR

THIS IS WHAT I LEARNED TODAY

TODAY'S PRAYER

Because thy lovingkindness is better than life, my lips shall praise thee. Psalm 63:3

DAY 28

TODAY I'M READING

GOD IS...

3 THINGS I'M THANKFUL FOR

THIS IS WHAT I LEARNED TODAY

TODAY'S PRAYER

Hatred stirreth up strifes: but love covereth all sins.
Proverbs 10:12

Smile!

DAY 29

TODAY I'M READING

GOD IS...

3 THINGS I'M THANKFUL FOR

THIS IS WHAT I LEARNED TODAY

TODAY'S PRAYER

A friend loveth at all times, and a brother is born for adversity. Proverbs 17:17

DAY 30

TODAY I'M READING

GOD IS...

3 THINGS I'M THANKFUL FOR

THIS IS WHAT I LEARNED TODAY

About the Author:

Darlene Schacht, is known by her readers as The Time-Warp Wife. She's is an Evangelical Christian whose number one priority is to serve Jesus Christ in every area of her life. She and her husband Michael live in Manitoba Canada. Married 26 years, they have four children (three still at home) and a pug.

Their lives are basically surrounded with three things: faith, music and everything books.

She's an award winning and New York Times best-selling author through a book she co-authored with actress Candace Cameron Bure, Reshaping it All.

Her articles have been featured at KirkCameron.com, FortheFamily.Org, and WomenLivingWell.org

Find Darlene on the web here:

Blog: TimeWarpWife.com Facebook: timewarpwife

Twitter: timewarpwife Pinterest: timewarpwife

If you enjoyed this book, please leave a review at Amazon. Thank you!

52812970R00038

Made in the USA
Lexington, KY
10 June 2016